CHRISTOPHER
COLUMBUS
EXPLORER OF THE
NEW WORLD

Portuguese traders importing slaves from Africa

The *Pinta*

The royal treasurer begs Queen Isabella of Spain to back Columbus's voyage.

Columbus lands at San Salvador.

CHRISTOPHER
COLUMBUS
EXPLORER OF THE
NEW WORLD

Written by
PETER CHRISP
Illustrated by
PETER DENNIS

A Dorling Kindersley Book

Dorling DK Kindersley

LONDON, NEW YORK, SYDNEY, DELHI, PARIS,
MUNICH, and JOHANNESBURG

Project Editor Steve Setford
Art Editor Peter Radcliffe
Senior Editor Marie Greenwood
Senior Art Editor Carole Oliver
Managing Art Editor Jacquie Gulliver
Publishing Manager Jayne Parsons
DTP Designer Nomazwe Madonko
Picture Researchers Amanda Russell, Pernilla Pearce,
and Marie Osborn
Jacket Designer Dean Price
Production Kate Oliver, Jenny Jacoby

Additional illustrations by David Ashby

First published in Great Britain in 2001 by
Dorling Kindersley Limited,
9 Henrietta Street,
Covent Garden, London WC2E 8PS

2 4 6 8 10 9 7 5 3 1

A CIP catalogue record for this book is available
from the British Library.

ISBN 0 7513 1388 2

Reproduced by Colourscan, Singapore
Printed and bound by L.E.G.O., Italy

For Lisa

see our complete
catalogue at
WWW.dk.com

Contents

The Age of Exploration

UNTIL THE EARLY 1400S, Europeans knew little about the wider world. But everything changed in the 15th century, when the kingdom of Portugal began to send ships out on voyages of exploration. Portuguese explorers worked their way down the western coast of Africa, establishing trading posts as they went, and found a route into the Indian Ocean.

> " This is the story of heroes who, leaving their native Portugal behind them, opened a way to Ceylon [Sri Lanka], and further, across seas no man had ever sailed before. "
>
> Luis de Camoens
> (Portuguese poet)
> *The Lusiads*, 1572

Portugal

The African coast, with names given by Portuguese explorers

World map by Henricus Martellus, c.1490

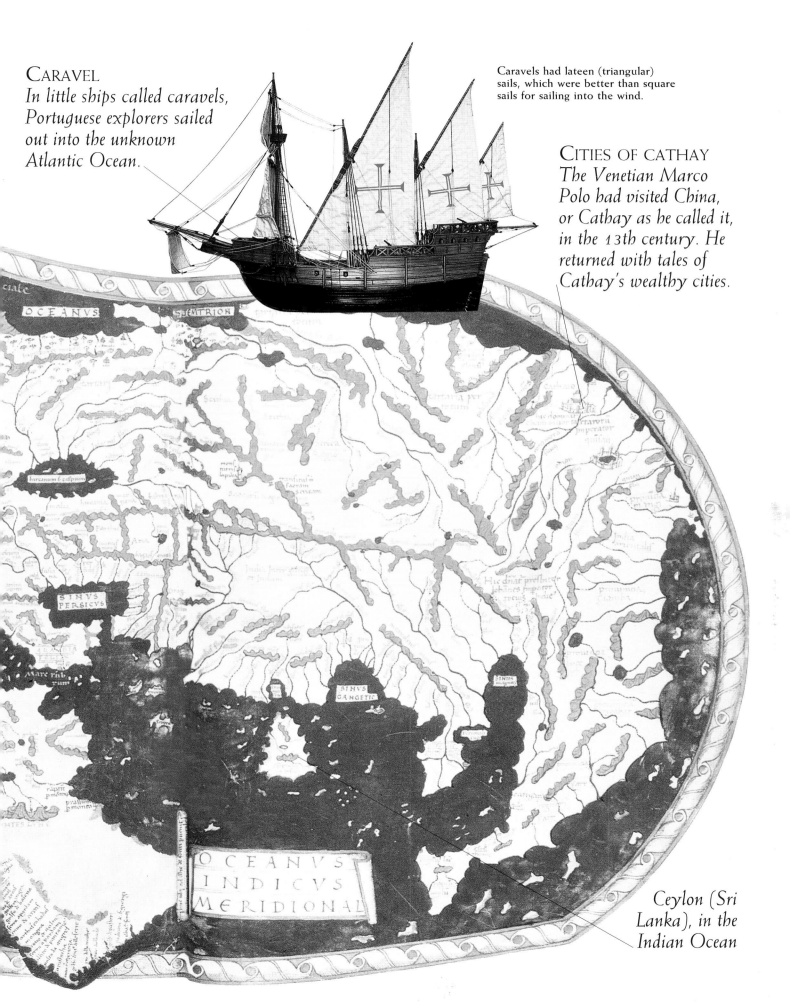

CARAVEL
In little ships called caravels, Portuguese explorers sailed out into the unknown Atlantic Ocean.

Caravels had lateen (triangular) sails, which were better than square sails for sailing into the wind.

CITIES OF CATHAY
The Venetian Marco Polo had visited China, or Cathay as he called it, in the 13th century. He returned with tales of Cathay's wealthy cities.

OCEANVS INDICVS MERIDIONAL

Ceylon (Sri Lanka), in the Indian Ocean

IN SEARCH OF THE INDIES

THE AIM OF THE EUROPEAN VOYAGES of exploration was to reach "the Indies", which was the old European name for Asia. The Indies included all the eastern lands, from India to Japan. Europeans had only the vaguest ideas of where these places were. The one thing they did know was that the Indies were rich. They had spices, gold, jewels, and silk – goods that were scarce in Europe, and which Europeans desperately wanted to get their hands on.

> **" Cipangu [Japan] has gold in measureless amounts. The island's ruler has a very large palace entirely roofed with fine gold. "**
>
> Marco Polo and Rusticello of Pisa, *The Travels of Marco Polo*, c.1299

Marco Polo journeyed all over Asia on missions for the Khan.

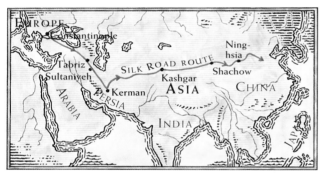

MARCO POLO
In the late 1200s, the merchant Marco Polo of Venice became one of the few Europeans to visit Asia. He took four years to travel the Silk Road to China, where he spent 17 years serving the emperor Kublai Khan as a diplomat.

THE SILK ROAD
For centuries, spices and other eastern goods had been brought west along a trade route called the Silk Road. By the time they reached Europe they were hugely expensive, because of the profits taken by all the merchants who bought and sold them along the way.

Spices such as cinnamon added exciting new flavours to European foods.

Silk Road goods

THE GOODS CARRIED WEST along the Silk Road came from all over Asia. Silk fabrics were made in China. Cinnamon came from Sri Lanka. India supplied black pepper.

Cinnamon

Cloves

Silk   Nutmeg   Black pepper

SPICE ISLANDS
The most expensive spices, including nutmeg and cloves, only grew in the "Spice Islands" (better known as the Moluccas) of eastern Indonesia.

FANTASTIC STORIES
On his return to Italy, Marco Polo's stories of the Indies were published as a book. It described Asian rivers full of precious stones (above), and many more fantastic sights. People loved his tales, but many readers thought he had made them up.

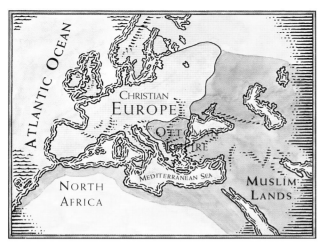

OTTOMAN EMPIRE
By the 15th century, the crusades had failed, and Europe was on the defensive. The Muslim Ottoman Turks launched their own holy war, sweeping through Greece and the Balkans, and conquering islands in the Mediterranean, such as Rhodes. The strength of the Ottoman Empire made it harder than ever for Europeans to reach the Indies overland.

Ottoman forces conquering Rhodes in 1522

NO ROUTE EAST
Christian Europe (pink) was hemmed in by Muslims, who ruled the lands to the south and east (green). There had been bitter hatred between the two religions since the 11th century, when the Christians began a series of holy wars, called crusades, against the Muslims.

Camels could carry heavier loads than horses or donkeys, and they were better suited to the harsh desert conditions encountered on the route.

CAMEL CARAVAN
Camels were the main pack animals used to carry goods along the Silk Road. They travelled in long lines called caravans.

Riding their short, stocky horses, the Khan's soldiers escorted Marco Polo on his missions.

Henry the Navigator
Prince Henry of Portugal, nicknamed Henry the Navigator, realized that the best way to get around the Muslim barrier was by sea. In the early 1400s, he sent a series of expeditions down the coast of Africa. Henry had started the age of European exploration.

FACT file

• Marco Polo dictated his stories to a writer named Rusticello while serving a prison sentence in Genoa.

• His book claimed that the Chinese burned black stones for fuel. His European readers, who did not know about coal, found this hard to believe.

• On his death bed, Marco Polo was asked if he had made up his stories. He replied that he had not recorded half of what he had seen in the Indies.

• Other travellers' tales told of giant gold-mining ants, and headless people, whose faces were on their chests.

Prester John

PRINCE HENRY HAD HEARD travellers' tales of a powerful Christian king called Prester John, who ruled somewhere in Africa or Asia. He hoped that the Portuguese voyages of exploration would find Prester John, so that he could help Christian Europe fight a new crusade against the Muslims.

Imaginary king
Although he was pictured on maps, Prester John did not really exist.

CHRISTOPHER COLUMBUS

BORN IN GENOA, NORTHERN ITALY, IN 1451, Christopher Columbus decided at an early age that he wanted to go to sea, rather than follow in his father's footsteps as a weaver and wool merchant. By his mid-teens, Columbus was sailing on merchant voyages all around the Mediterranean Sea. He had little formal education, but showed a natural skill as a navigator. Aged 25, he moved to Portugal. For a young man curious to find out about the world, Portugal in the age of exploration was the ideal place to be.

Engraving of Genoa harbour
Columbus's home city, Genoa, was one of the Mediterranean's busiest ports. As a boy, Columbus must have watched hundreds of merchant ships arriving and departing, and dreamed of a life of adventure as a sailor.

Into the Atlantic
Columbus sailed on several trading voyages out into the Atlantic Ocean from Lisbon. He sailed north to Iceland, and south to Guinea, all the while learning about the great ocean and its system of winds and currents.

LISBON DOCKS
Columbus settled in the Portuguese capital, Lisbon, built beside the wide River Tagus, which pours into the Atlantic Ocean. At the docks, the air resounded with a babble of different languages as sailors from many lands loaded and unloaded cargo from ships.

COLUMBUS THE SEAMAN
As an experienced navigator, Columbus was always welcome at the bustling dockside.

EUROPEAN EXPORTS
Portuguese ships sailed to Africa with cargoes of horses, glass beads, brass bells, carpets, English wool, and Irish linen.

SHIPWRECKED
A shipwreck first brought Columbus to Portugal. In 1476, he sailed with a Genoese fleet, which was attacked by French warships off the Portuguese coast. Columbus's ship sank, but he made it safely ashore.

Columbus saved himself by clinging on to a floating oar.

Navigating in known waters

COLUMBUS LEARNED TO FIND HIS WAY at sea using a magnetic compass and a map called a portolan, which was marked with criss-cross lines. When sailing in known waters, a mariner could use these two navigational tools to plot a course between any two ports.

Compass
A compass has a magnetic needle that always points towards north.

Portolan map
When drawing a portolan, a mapmaker used a grid of criss-cross lines as a guide for accuracy. The lines also helped a navigator to find the sailing direction and distance from port to port.

> " At a very tender age, I went to sea sailing, and so I have continued to this day. The art of navigation leads the man who follows it to want to know the secrets of this world. "
>
> Christopher Columbus, from a letter to the king and queen of Spain, 1501

GOLD COAST TRADE
The Portuguese found a rich source of gold in part of Guinea, West Africa, which they called "the Gold Coast". Gold from here was brought to Lisbon, where it was made into coins called *cruzados* ("crusades").

RICH REWARDS
Columbus sailed to Guinea on a ship like this. Deeply impressed by the gold mines he saw, he realized how profitable voyages of exploration could be.

CAPTIVE CONVERTS
The Portuguese saw nothing wrong in enslaving non-Christians. They made the slaves convert to Christianity, believing that they would benefit by learning about the "true faith".

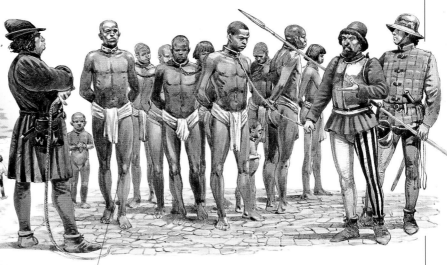

Sugar cane from Madeira

AFRICAN IMPORTS
Ships arriving from Africa unloaded slaves, chests of gold dust, bundles of ivory, and barrels full of a pepper-like spice called malagueta.

In Africa, these 11 slaves could have been bought in exchange for a single horse.

IMPORTING SLAVES
Between 1450 and 1500, around 150,000 African slaves passed through the Lisbon docks. The Portuguese bought them from local slave traders and African chiefs. There was frequent warfare between the chiefs, who often raided each other's territories to take prisoners whom they could sell as slaves.

> 66 The Earth is round. Six parts of the globe can be lived upon, the seventh is covered with water...Between the end of Spain and the beginning of India lies a narrow sea that can be sailed in a few days with a favourable wind. 99
>
> Cardinal Pierre d'Ailly,
> *Imago Mundi*,
> 1410

THE PLAN

AS HE SAILED ON TRADING VOYAGES in the Atlantic Ocean, Christopher Columbus must have often gazed at the western horizon, and wondered what secrets it held. This was still a mysterious ocean. Nobody knew how wide it was, or what you would find if you tried to sail across it. Columbus had read Marco Polo's stories of the gold-roofed palace of Cipangu and the wealth of the Great Khan of Cathay. It struck him that these rich lands must lie on the other side of the Atlantic, and that it might be possible to reach them by sailing west. So Columbus began to work out a plan to sail across the Atlantic Ocean, and find the riches of the Indies.

Imago Mundi

COLUMBUS FOUND SUPPORT for his plan in *Imago Mundi* ("Picture of the World"), a geography book written by a French cardinal, Pierre d'Ailly. The cardinal had read in the ancient Jewish book of Esdras that sea covered only one-seventh of the Earth's surface. From this, d'Ailly argued that the Atlantic could not be a wide ocean.

Columbus covered his copy of Imago Mundi with notes in different inks, showing that he read it many times.

Columbus always kept his copies of Imago Mundi *and Marco Polo's* Travels *beside him as he worked.*

EVIDENCE
Columbus studied geography books to find evidence that his voyage was possible. He calculated the size of Europe and Asia and the distance around the Earth. Using only writers who would back up his ideas, he tried to prove that the Atlantic was a narrow sea.

A skilled mapmaker, Columbus drew charts to show that his plan was practical.

TOSCANELLI
Columbus learned that, in 1474, Italian scholar Paolo Toscanelli had tried to convince the Portuguese king to back a western sea voyage to Asia. Columbus wrote to Toscanelli, who sent him a sea chart and a letter encouraging him in his "great and noble desire".

BIBLE

As a strong Christian, Columbus believed that all important knowledge was in the Bible, which was thought to be the word of God. The only continents mentioned in the Bible are Europe, Africa, and Asia, so he would have had no inkling that the Americas existed.

Columbus's namesake, Saint Christopher, was the patron saint of seafarers and travellers.

A deeply religious man, Columbus often read the Bible.

Columbus probably used a crucifix and rosary beads as prayer aids.

SAINT CHRISTOPHER

The name Christopher means "Christ bearer". It comes from the saint who, in legend, carried a child safely across a river. The child then revealed that he was Jesus Christ. Columbus felt that he was a new Saint Christopher, chosen by God to carry Christianity across the sea to the Indies.

MARTIN BEHAIM

The German geographer Martin Behaim pictured the world in a similar way to Columbus. He, too, dreamed of making a western sea voyage to the Indies. Although Behaim was in Portugal at the same time as Columbus, there is no evidence that the two men ever met.

BEHAIM'S GLOBE
In 1492, Martin Behaim built a globe to show that a westward sea voyage to the Indies was possible. Behaim's is the oldest surviving globe in the world today.

Copy of Behaim's 1492 globe

Mapping the Earth

ALL EDUCATED PEOPLE knew that the world was round, but there were arguments about its size, and how much of it was covered by water. Many scholars believed that the Atlantic stretched over half the globe. Columbus rejected this idea, as it made his voyage unthinkable.

Columbus's world
Columbus assumed that there was only the open water of the Atlantic between Spain and Asia. He also thought that there were many islands off the coast of Asia, where he could break his journey.

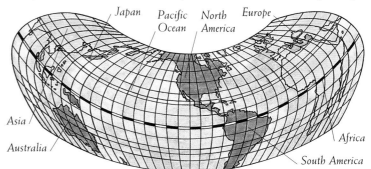

The true picture
Columbus misjudged the size of the Earth, believing it to be much smaller than it really is. There are huge continents, the Americas, where Columbus hoped to find Asia, and another, Australia, below Asia. A huge ocean, called the Pacific, separates the Americas from Asia.

THE QUEST FOR A ROYAL SPONSOR

COLUMBUS COULD NOT SAIL ON his voyage without royal backing. He wanted to arrive in the Indies as the ambassador of a powerful king, and he needed the king's money to pay for all the ships, crews, and supplies. Columbus was also very ambitious and expected to be rewarded for his discoveries by being made a noble. So, in 1484, he approached King John II of Portugal, and explained his plan. The king did not believe in Marco Polo's tales of Cipangu (Japan), so he turned Columbus down. In any case, John was far more interested in the wealth his ships were already bringing back from their trips to Africa.

AUDIENCE WITH THE QUEEN

After being rejected in Portugal, Columbus moved to Spain in 1485 to seek sponsorship from King Ferdinand and Queen Isabella. A year later, Isabella met with Columbus in Cordova and listened to his plan with interest.

Reconquest

FERDINAND AND ISABELLA WERE BUSY fighting, and winning, a war against the Muslim Moors, who ruled southern Spain. Only after the fall of Granada, the last Muslim stronghold, on 2 January 1492, could they give their full attention to Columbus's proposal.

Arms of Leon and Castille

BEFORE THE COMMISSION

Ferdinand and Isabella knew little about geography or voyages of exploration, so they appointed a commission of experts to see if Columbus's plan made sense. The experts were mostly churchmen, along with some scholars and seamen.

PRESENTING THE PLAN
Columbus explained his plan to the royal experts. To support his ideas, he showed them his map of the Atlantic, and read to them from his favourite books on geography.

Woodcut of Ferdinand, commemorating the conquest of Granada in 1492

Coat of arms of Granada

Santangel told Isabella she was wrong to reject Columbus.

Return to Portugal

IN 1488, WHILE AWAITING THE EXPERTS' DECISION, Columbus decided to try his luck again in Portugal. He arrived in time to see the triumphant return of explorer Bartolomeu Dias, who had just found a way around the southern tip, or cape, of Africa into the Indian Ocean.

Hope and gloom
The cape Dias found was named "Good Hope". Dias had opened up an eastern sea route to the Indies. The Portuguese now had no use for Columbus, so he gloomily made his way back to Spain.

Dias set up a cross on the cape to claim the land for Portugal.

FRIEND AT COURT
Luis de Santangel, the royal treasurer, was a friend of Columbus. Santangel told Isabella that Columbus's plan would bring Spain wealth and glory, and help to spread the Christian religion. He warned that Spain would lose out if a rival kingdom sponsored the voyage instead.

FINANCING THE TRIP
Santangel had so much faith in Columbus that he offered to pay for the voyage himself. Won over by Santangel, Isabella said she would raise the money for the trip, even if it meant pawning her jewels.

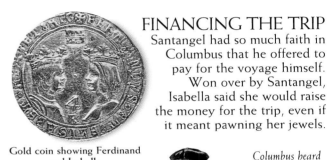

Gold coin showing Ferdinand and Isabella

THE EXPERTS DECIDE
The experts concluded that Columbus's ideas were mistaken, and that it would take at least three years to sail west to Asia. Isabella and Ferdinand were also put off by Columbus's demands – he wanted to rule as viceroy over any lands that he discovered. In January 1492, after six-and-a-half years, Columbus was rejected once again.

The experts were not convinced by Columbus's calculations.

Columbus heard the good news from a royal messenger.

COLUMBUS CALLED BACK
Meanwhile, Columbus packed his belongings and set off for France, intent on offering his plan to yet another king. But before long, a messenger caught up with Columbus and told him that the queen had changed her mind. He would sail to the Indies after all!

SHIPS AND CREW

ON 12 MAY 1492, COLUMBUS TRAVELLED

to the port of Palos, on the south coast of Spain, to prepare for his voyage to the Indies. The people of Palos had upset Ferdinand and Isabella in some way, now unknown. As punishment, they were ordered to supply Columbus with two ships, *Niña* and *Pinta*. Columbus hired a third ship, *Santa Maria*, from his friend Juan de la Cosa. Getting the ships was the easy part. Now Columbus had to find more than 90 men and boys to crew his three ships.

Santa Maria
Ships had an official name, usually that of a saint, and a female nickname. Columbus's flagship, *Santa Maria*, was nicknamed *La Gallega* ("the Galician") after Galicia in northern Spain, where she was made. A *não*, or round-bellied cargo ship, she was the slowest vessel in the fleet, and the hardest to handle.

The anchor was raised and lowered on a long thick rope that ran through this hole.

EAGLE-EYES
Lookouts stood forward and at the mast-head, their eyes scouring the seas for signs of land.

INSIDE SANTA MARIA
For four months, *Santa Maria* would be home to a crew of more than 40 men and boys – together with cockroaches, rats, lice, and fleas! Columbus had his own cabin, but everyone else slept in the open air, on deck. The areas below deck were too smelly and cramped.

Falconet

WEAPONS
Columbus did not know if the people of the Indies would be peaceful or hostile, so the ships had small, swivelling guns called falconets, as well as larger cannons called lombards. The men were armed with swords, crossbows, and muskets.

Spare sails

Meals were cooked above an open fire on a fogón (firebox).

Finding a crew
At first, nobody in Palos wanted to sail with Columbus. Spanish sailors did not want to risk their lives on a dangerous voyage into the unknown, captained by a foreigner. Columbus's plan struck them as insane.

Rowing boat

PUMP
Every day the men had to pump out water that leaked into the hold. All wooden ships leaked.

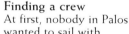

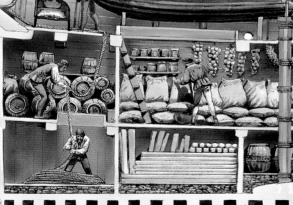

LIFE AT...

The men ... from of work, ... one half ... sailed the ... have voyage, ... other problem ... oute.

...w flags ...th the royal ...s of Spain.

...led on ...the ...ia.

2... Sep...

tha... wes... to ... Bu... ou...

Co... creu... be ... bac... to t...

"I have decided to set down each day full details of everything I do, see, and experience on this voyage…Above all, I must have no regard for sleep, but must carefully watch my course. All of this will be no small task."

Christopher Columbus,
extract from his logbook of
the voyage, 1492

19th-century painting of
Columbus's fleet

The little Niña, captained
by Vincente Yáñez Pinzón,
set off with lateen sails.

THE MEN FROM THE SKY

" EYEWITNESS
We understood them to be asking if we had come from the sky. One old man climbed into the boat while the other men and women shouted 'come and see the men who have come from the sky!' **"**

Christopher Columbus, extract from his logbook of the first voyage, 1492

COLUMBUS HAD ARRIVED AT THE islands we now know as the Bahamas, which were home to the Taino people. The Tainos were amazed to see strange, bearded men who covered their bodies with clothes. They thought that the Spaniards had come down from the sky. Once they had got over their fear, the Tainos were eager to please the strangers. Columbus decided that these "Indians" would make fine servants.

Columbus knew that, back in Spain, the Tainos would make a big impression on Ferdinand and Isabella.

Two of the captives later escaped. The rest would never see their homes again.

IN THE VILLAGES
Columbus travelled from island to island, visiting Taino villages. Some of the villages were more like towns, with up to 1,000 huts and 5,000 inhabitants.

Cotton was woven to make loincloths and hammocks.

The Tainos were skilled at pottery.

Grinding maize to make porridge

Capturing guides
Although Columbus was pleased to reach land at last, it was clearly not Japan. Where were the buildings roofed with gold? To find Japan, he needed guides, so he captured seven Tainos and took them back to his ships.

New foods

EVERYTHING IN THE ISLANDS was new and strange to Columbus. His men were the first Europeans to enjoy many foods, such as maize, which we now take for granted. But they avoided other Taino foods, such as lizards, spiders, and worms.

Cassava root
The Tainos made poisonous cassava roots edible by grating and soaking them. Dried cassava was baked into bread.

Pineapple
This was one of the few Taino foods that the Spaniards liked as soon as they tried it.

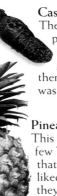

Maize
Maize was roasted and eaten whole, or ground up to make a kind of porridge.

Chilli peppers
Hot chillies reminded Columbus of the spices he hoped to find in the Indies, which is why we call them "peppers" today.

The Taino culture

THE TAINOS WORSHIPPED A GREAT SPIRIT who lived in the sky, where they thought Columbus had come from. They believed that, on Earth, they were surrounded by other spirits, called zemis. Some were forces of nature, while others were the ghosts of ancestors.

Their foreheads were flattened as babies, when boards were strapped to them.

Decoration
Instead of wearing clothes, the Tainos painted their bodies in different colours and patterns. In their pierced noses and ears they wore gold or stone jewellery.

Tall homes
Taino homes were huts made of wooden poles, with cane walls and tall, sloping roofs thatched with palm leaves.

Some zemis were roughly shaped stones, others were beautiful carvings.

Zemis
People kept small carved or pottery figures of the zemis in their huts, so that the spirits would protect their homes.

The Tainos had no hard metals, so they tipped their arrows and spears with fish teeth.

WHICH WAY TO JAPAN? None of the Tainos had ever heard of Cipangu (Japan) or the Great Khan of Cathay.

The Spaniards received a warm and excited welcome. They gave the Tainos woollen hats and glass beads to wear.

The bells were made for the legs of hunting hawks.

Brass for gold
Columbus's most popular trade goods were little brass bells. The Tainos were eager to trade their gold nose ornaments for these bells, which they wore as earrings. Columbus was disappointed to find that the Tainos had only tiny amounts of gold, and that the ornaments were wafer thin.

Each canoe was hollowed out from a single tree trunk.

THEY MUST BE INDIANS
Believing he was in the Indies, Columbus naturally assumed that the islanders were Indians. He could see that they were not Europeans or Africans. As far as he knew, this was what Asian people looked like. Columbus's mistake means that, to this day, Native Americans are still called "Indians".

*SILENT DOGS
The Tainos kept dogs, which they fattened and ate. The Spaniards were surprised to find that Taino dogs never barked.*

Taino canoes
Columbus sailed through the islands, giving each one a new Spanish name, and claiming them all for Spain. As news of his arrival spread, many Tainos came out in their canoes to see the "men from the sky". They brought colourful parrots, balls of cotton, bows and arrows, and other goods to trade.

SHIPWRECKED IN HISPANIOLA

COLUMBUS'S GUIDES TOLD HIM OF A LARGE island to the south that they called Cuba. Thinking that this might be Japan, he sailed to Cuba, but again found no golden palaces. However, the friendly Cuban Tainos said there was another island to the east, called Haiti, which was rich in gold. On 6 December 1492, Columbus reached Haiti. He was amazed by its beauty and relieved that the local Tainos seemed to have plenty of gold ornaments. He gave the island a new name, La Isla Española ("the Spanish Island"), which later became Hispaniola.

Columbus outraged
On 21 November, when the fleet was heading south along the Cuban coast, *Pinta* suddenly sailed off to the east. Tired of obeying Columbus, Martín Pinzón had decided to go exploring on his own. Columbus was furious that Pinzón had deserted the fleet, taking the fastest ship with him.

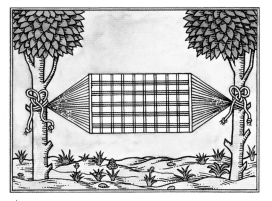

Hammocks
The Tainos slept in long cotton nets slung from the posts of their houses. These hanging beds were known as *hamaca*. The idea would later be adopted for use on ships by European sailors, who called them hammocks.

RUN AGROUND!
On Christmas Eve (24 December) 1492, *Santa Maria* ran aground on rocks off the coast of Hispaniola. All efforts to refloat her failed. When holes opened up in the hull, which began to fill with water, Columbus gave the order to abandon ship.

Everything that might be useful was stripped from the ship.

Tobacco leaves were rolled into cigars.

Drinking the smoke of herbs
The Spaniards were amazed to see Cuban Tainos "drinking" the smoke of rolled up leaves. They were smoking tobacco. The Tainos also inhaled the smoke through a wooden tube, called a *tobaco*, inserted into one nostril.

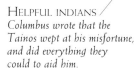

HELPFUL INDIANS
Columbus wrote that the Tainos wept at his misfortune, and did everything they could to aid him.

SALVAGE MISSION
The next day, the crew returned to their ship to salvage as much as possible. They unloaded stores and trading goods into the rowing boats from Santa Maria and Niña.

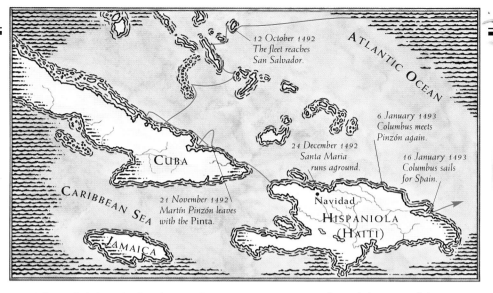

12 October 1492
The fleet reaches
San Salvador.

ATLANTIC OCEAN

6 January 1493
Columbus meets
Pinzón again.

24 December 1492
Santa Maria
runs aground.

16 January 1493
Columbus sails
for Spain.

CUBA

CARIBBEAN SEA

21 November 1492
Martín Pinzón leaves
with the Pinta.

Navidad

HISPANIOLA
(HAITI)

JAMAICA

AMONG THE ISLANDS

Columbus explored the north coast of Cuba, which he believed was part of the Asian mainland. Then he crossed over to Hispaniola (Haiti). Martín Pinzón had got there first, and had even named a river after himself – the River Martín Alonso.

Pinzón's desertion and the wreck of Santa Maria *left Columbus with just one ship,* Niña, *so Columbus could not risk further exploration.*

The fort was built using timbers from the wrecked Santa Maria.

A wooden stockade protected the men's home.

Santa Maria *did not sink, but remained stranded on the rocks.*

Many Tainos rowed out in their long canoes to help the crew unload the ship's supplies.

BUILDING A SETTLEMENT

Niña was too small to take all the men back to Spain, so 39 of them volunteered to stay behind. To house the men, Columbus built a fort – the first European settlement in the Americas. It was called Navidad ("Christmas"), since it was begun on Christmas Day 1492. Columbus promised to return in a few months with supplies. The men were happy to stay, believing they would get rich on Hispaniola's gold.

The Tainos were terrified by the noise as the cannon blasted shots through the wreck of Santa Maria.

SHOW OF STRENGTH

The Tainos told Columbus about a fierce people – the Caribs – who regularly raided their island for captives to kill and eat. Columbus said they now had nothing to fear, since the Spaniards at Navidad would protect them from the Caribs. To impress the Tainos, he fired a cannon at a farewell feast. *Niña* set sail for Spain on 4 January 1493.

TIME TO GO HOME

Looking at his wrecked flagship *Santa Maria*, Columbus realized that it was time to return home to Spain. He needed to tell Ferdinand and Isabella about the lands he had discovered. He did not want Martín Pinzón to get there first and steal his glory.

> ❝ The Catholic sovereigns, surrounded by their court, awaited him on a magnificent throne under a golden canopy. When he came to kiss their hands, they stood up to greet him as if he were a great lord, and sat him beside them. ❞
>
> Ferdinand Columbus,
> *The Life of the Admiral,*
> 1530s

TRIUMPHANT HOMECOMING

AFTER A STORMY RETURN JOURNEY across the Atlantic Ocean, Columbus reached Palos in Spain on 15 March 1493. He then travelled overland to Barcelona, where Ferdinand and Isabella gave him a magnificent royal reception. Sadly for Martín Pinzón, it was a very different homecoming. On board *Pinta*, Pinzón got back to Spain first, but the king and queen refused to see him without Columbus. Pinzón went home to Palos, where he is said to have died of grief.

ROYAL RECEPTION

The king and queen welcomed Columbus in the great hall of their palace. With his captured Tainos and colourful parrots, Columbus put on a show to impress them. He explained how he wanted to return to Hispaniola and build a Spanish colony.

Vividly coloured parrots were additional proof that Columbus had been to the Indies.

Message in a barrel
On the return journey, the sea was so rough that Columbus thought *Niña* might sink. He was worried that if he died, Martín Pinzón, on *Pinta*, would steal his glory and the men left in Hispaniola would be forgotten. So he wrote an account of the voyage, placed it in a barrel, and threw it over the side.

Hero's welcome
The news of Columbus's great achievement reached Barcelona before he did. His arrival, in April 1493, caused a sensation. As he rode through the streets, everyone came out to gaze at the man who had found a sea route to the Indies. Columbus was acclaimed a hero.

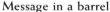

Statue of Columbus by Barcelona's harbour, commemorating his great discovery

The Tainos said "Ave Maria", a prayer honouring the Virgin Mary, which Columbus had taught them.

To the Tainos, the court was an astonishing sight.

Columbus presented gold, chillies, and other souvenirs of his 'ong trip.

"Admiral of the Ocean Sea"

FERDINAND AND ISABELLA richly rewarded Columbus with money and titles. As they had promised, they made him a noble. He was now "Admiral of the Ocean Sea, Viceroy and Governor of the Islands". Columbus had the right to rule Hispaniola on their behalf and to take a share of its wealth for himself.

Coat of arms
Columbus was allowed to have his own coat of arms. It combined images of the royal lion and castle of Spain with the islands he had discovered. It also included five golden anchors, which represented his new position as Admiral of the Ocean Sea.

Columbus, "Christ bearer"
After his return, Columbus began to sign all his documents with a strange group of letters. The first three lines remain a mystery. The last line says "Christ bearer" in Greek and Latin.

DESCRIBING HISPANIOLA
Columbus described the beauty of Hispaniola. He showed the king and queen the Taino gold he had collected, saying it was just a tiny sample of the vast wealth of the island.

NEW VOYAGE APPROVED
Ferdinand agreed at once to Columbus's plan to return to Hispaniola with a great fleet.

Isabella was especially moved by the sight of the gentle Tainos.

QUIZZED BY THE COURT
The king, queen, and members of the royal court plied Columbus with all manner of questions about his eight-month long voyage.

BAPTISM OF INDIANS
This plaque in Barcelona Cathedral commemorates the baptism of the captured Tainos. The king and queen acted as their godparents, and gave them new Spanish Christian names. Isabella was delighted to see them become Christian.

THE POPE'S BACKING
Columbus had claimed the Caribbean islands for Spain. To make their ownership legal, Ferdinand and Isabella needed the backing of Pope Alexander VI. The pope was happy to give it. Although unaware of it, the Tainos had become Spanish subjects.

The Spanish Settlement

> " Hispaniola is a wonder. The mountains, hills, plains, and meadows are fertile and beautiful. They are most suitable for planting crops and for all kinds of cattle, and there are good sites for building towns and villages... There are many great rivers, and most contain gold. "
>
> Christopher Columbus, from a letter written on his first voyage, 15 February 1493

IN SEPTEMBER 1493, JUST SIX MONTHS AFTER HIS triumphant homecoming, Columbus sailed back to Hispaniola. He had a grand fleet of 17 ships, carrying more than 1,200 men, as well as horses, sheep, pigs, seeds, and everything else he needed to build a Spanish settlement in the Indies. This time, Columbus had no trouble finding the men to sail with him. Thousands of Spaniards volunteered, eager to share in the wealth of Hispaniola. They included gentlemen, priests, soldiers, craftsmen, and labourers.

NAVIDAD
This 1493 woodcut shows Columbus's men constructing the fort of Navidad during his first voyage. Columbus hoped to build his new settlement around the fort.

The artist did not know what Navidad or Hispaniola looked like, so he drew a typical European landscape and castle.

The great fleet
This picture shows Columbus's fleet of colonizers setting off from Spain, with Ferdinand and Isabella saying goodbye. The Tainos had been amazed by the sight of Columbus's three ships on his first voyage. Imagine how they felt when they now saw 17 ships arriving!

COLUMBUS RETURNS

ON 27 NOVEMBER 1493, Columbus returned to Navidad, where he had left behind 39 men at the end of his first voyage. He was looking forward to a happy reunion with them, and was certain that by now they would have collected heaps of gold. Columbus was horrified to learn that they were all dead, and that their fort had been destroyed. The local Tainos said that they were not to blame, but Columbus could no longer trust them. He sailed east, to found a new settlement.

FATE OF NAVIDAD

The Tainos told Columbus that the men of Navidad had quarrelled among themselves, splitting into rival groups. Some were killed by fellow Spaniards, while others died of disease. But most died when a powerful cacique (king), called Caonabo, attacked their fort and burned it to the ground.

Some important buildings were made of stone, but the Spaniards mostly lived in small thatched huts.

Caonabo led a surprise attack at night.

Cannibal islands
On the way to Hispaniola, Columbus visited the islands of the fierce Caribs, who gave their name to the Caribbean and to the word "cannibal". Historians still argue over whether they really ate human flesh. Columbus was sure that they did: in their houses, he saw human limbs in cooking pots and captive Tainos who were being fattened up.

THE SECOND VOYAGE

While the settlers tried to get used to life on Hispaniola, Columbus set off exploring again in April 1494 on trusty *Niña*. He sailed along the south coast of Cuba, which he still thought was the Asian mainland, and reached Jamaica. But he found no signs of the wealth of Asia. In September, he became seriously ill. Suffering from fever and temporary blindness, he returned to Hispaniola a disappointed man.

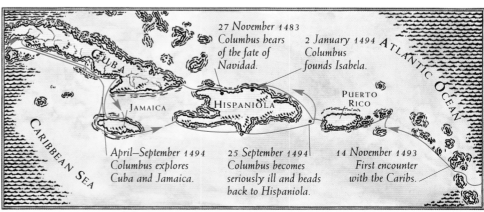

27 November 1483 Columbus hears of the fate of Navidad.

2 January 1494 Columbus founds Isabela.

ATLANTIC OCEAN

CUBA

JAMAICA

HISPANIOLA

PUERTO RICO

CARIBBEAN SEA

April–September 1494 Columbus explores Cuba and Jamaica.

25 September 1494 Columbus becomes seriously ill and heads back to Hispaniola.

14 November 1493 First encounter with the Caribs.

A trade in diseases

THE SPANIARDS and the Tainos each passed on unfamiliar diseases to the other, with devastating effect. Many Spaniards caught tropical fevers and syphilis, while the Tainos died from smallpox and measles.

Smallpox virus
The smallpox virus travelled to Hispaniola as an invisible passenger on Columbus's ships. In Europe, it killed many children, but most adults were immune to it. For the Tainos, it was fatal.

Mosquitoes
A week after arriving, 400 Spanish settlers became ill with an unknown disease, probably caused by mosquito bites. There were so many mosquitoes in Isabela that Columbus was nicknamed, "Admiral of the Mosquitoes".

Female mosquitoes pass on tropical fevers as they feed on blood.

Flamingoes
While exploring the tiny islands off Cuba, Columbus marvelled at the sight of masses of brightly coloured wading birds. From a distance, they looked like flocks of pink sheep. These were flamingoes, named after the Spanish word *flamenco* ("flaming").

ISABELA
Columbus called his new capital Isabela, in honour of the queen. He chose the location in the mistaken belief that there were gold mines nearby. It was an unhealthy, mosquito-infested place. By 1500, Isabela had been abandoned.

FIRST CHURCH
The church of Isabela was the first built in the Americas. The sound of its bell fascinated the Hispaniola Tainos.

Columbus planned Isabela around a main public square, like a typical Spanish town.

Taino guides led the Spanish explorers inland.

Taino caciques
Hispaniola was made up of several kingdoms, each ruled by a great king, or cacique (pronounced "katheekay"). There were also many lesser caciques, ruling the villages. Caciques were treated with great respect and carried on litters. To govern Hispaniola, Columbus needed to win over the caciques or defeat them in battle.

FACT file

• By 1494, two-thirds of the Spanish settlers in Isabela had died.

• In 1492, there were around 100 million Native Americans. By 1600, European diseases had killed 90 million of them – the worst disaster in history.

• One Spaniard wrote that the Indians "die so easily that the bare look and smell of a Spaniard makes them give up the ghost".

• A mild form of syphilis already existed in Europe, but the American version brought back by the Spaniards was far worse. The first mass outbreak of this disease was in Italy, in 1494.

INTO THE INTERIOR
Columbus was desperate to find gold to send back to Ferdinand and Isabella, in order to justify the expense of the colony. In January 1494, he sent a party of armed Spaniards inland to look for gold mines. They were led by a tough, aggressive soldier called Alonso de Hojeda.

HORROR ON HISPANIOLA

FOLLOWING HIS RETURN TO HISPANIOLA, in September 1494, Columbus was ill for five months. The colony was ruled by his younger brothers, Diego and Bartolomé, who had crossed the sea to share in their brother's fortune. As foreigners, all three brothers were unpopular with the Spaniards. The Spanish settlers also felt that Columbus had lied to them about the wealth of Hispaniola. While Columbus lay on his sickbed, gangs of discontented Spaniards were roaming around the island, living by plundering Taino villages. The Tainos began to fight back.

FACT file

- Between 1494 and 1496, a third of all the Tainos on Hispaniola died.
- Apart from the Tainos killed by the Spaniards, thousands died of disease, starvation, and overwork. Unable to cope with Spanish rule, others killed themselves by taking cassava poison.
- In 1492, there were some 300,000 Tainos on Hispaniola. By 1548, there were less than 500 left.
- In 1510, the Spaniards began to ship African slaves to Hispaniola, to replace the dwindling numbers of Tainos.

DECISIVE BATTLE

After recovering from illness, Columbus learned that the most powerful Taino caciques had joined together and raised a huge army, thousands strong. In March 1495, he set off to fight them. His 200 Spanish soldiers were vastly outnumbered, but they had superior weapons and devastated the Taino army.

THUNDER-STICKS
The battle began with the roar of musketeers firing their matchlock guns. To the Tainos, matchlocks were magic sticks that made thunder and spewed fire.

The Tainos were terrified by the sight of armoured Spaniards on horseback. They had never seen horses before.

Reign of terror
The Tainos reacted to raids on their villages by ambushing stray Spaniards. Columbus did not want to risk upsetting his men. Instead of punishing them for their brutal behaviour, he sent them on an expedition against the Tainos. Hundreds of Tainos were killed or brought back to Isabela as slaves.

SHIPMENT OF SLAVES

In 1495, Columbus sent 500 Taino slaves back to Spain. He hoped that these slaves would make up for his failure to send the gold he had promised. But the king and queen were not happy with Columbus's "gift" – they had sent him to convert the Tainos to Christianity, not to enslave them.

DEATH TOLL
Of the 500 Tainos that Columbus captured and sent to Spain, 200 perished during the voyage. The rest died soon after.

Arms and armour

THE SPANIARDS WERE EXPERT SOLDIERS, who had spent years fighting Muslim armies in Spain. Equipped with swords and guns, the Spaniards saw little reason to fear the poorly armed Tainos.

Cavalry helmet
Helmets similar to this one made the Spaniards look like monsters from another world.

Matchlock gun
A matchlock was fired by bringing a burning cord, or match, into contact with gunpowder.

Sword
Spanish swords were double edged for slashing, and had a sharp point for stabbing.

Breastplate
Taino arrows and spears were useless against steel breastplates.

Crossbow
A crossbow fired a bolt with great force, seriously injuring any Taino it hit.

Some brave Tainos tried to fight back, but they could do little damage with their fishbone-tipped spears.

DOGS OF WAR
One Spanish dog was said to be as good as ten men in a fight against Indians.

Naked Tainos had no defence against the terrible Spanish weapons.

Indians bringing gold tributes to the Spaniards

GOLD TRIBUTE
The conquered Tainos were ordered to give their new rulers gold as tribute. Every three months, each adult Taino was expected to fill one hawk's bell with gold dust. Unfortunately, there was much less gold in Hispaniola than this picture suggests. The Tainos could never find enough to please the Spaniards.

The Tainos fled in all directions.

Columbus returns to Spain
Disgruntled settlers returning to Spain complained to Ferdinand and Isabella about the way Columbus ruled Hispaniola. In March 1496, Columbus sailed back to Spain in *Niña*, in order to defend himself.

CONQUERING HISPANIOLA
Columbus went on to conquer the whole island. The cacique Caonabo, who had burned the fort at Navidad, was captured by Alonso de Hojeda. Hojeda tricked Caonabo into letting himself be chained up by convincing him that some handcuffs and leg-irons were royal bracelets.

Before leaving, Columbus appointed his brother Bartolomé as governor.

To the Mainland

> I made a new voyage to new skies and lands which had been hidden until now…By my efforts, these lands are now known. "
>
> Christopher Columbus, from a letter to Juana de la Torre, Queen Isabella's friend, 1500

ON HIS THIRD VOYAGE, IN 1498, COLUMBUS FOUND A LONG coastline, broken by the mouth of a mighty river whose water made the sea taste fresh for miles around. Such a great river could not flow from an island. Columbus realized that he had reached a mainland. This mainland would later be known as South America.

Just off the mainland, Columbus found a large island, which he named Trinidad in honour of the Holy Trinity (God as Father, Son, and Holy Spirit).

Sixteenth-century woodcut depicting scenes from the third voyage

Columbus's fleet sailed between Trinidad and the mainland.

The mainland Indians wore pearls, which they fished for by diving from their canoes.

ANOTHER WORLD

THE KING AND QUEEN WERE WORRIED BY events in Hispaniola, but they had not yet lost faith in Columbus. They agreed to pay for a third voyage of exploration, which set off in May 1498. Columbus was amazed to find a mainland, which he described as "another world". After exploring part of its coast, he returned to Hispaniola. He found the island in a state of chaos: half the Spaniards had rebelled against his brother, Bartolomé.

EYEWITNESS

"I have come to believe that this is a vast continent, previously unknown. I am led to this view by the great river and the fresh-water sea. If this be a continent, it is a marvellous thing."

Christopher Columbus,
journal of his third voyage,
14/15 August
1498

Giant wave
Off the coast of Trinidad, Columbus's ships were almost wrecked by a giant wave, possibly caused by an undersea volcano. The wave lifted the ships high into the air, and then plunged them so low that they could see the bottom.

Audience of monkeys
On 5 August 1498, Columbus landed on the mainland. To legally claim the land for Spain, he needed an audience of local people. The only inhabitants he found were chattering monkeys, so he put off the ceremony until the next day, when some friendly Indians turned up.

THE THIRD VOYAGE
Columbus's exploration of the mainland was cut short by a fresh bout of illness. Returning to Hispaniola, he reached Santa Domingo, the island's new capital, on 31 August 1498. His brother Bartolomé had founded Santa Domingo to replace the mosquito-infested Isabela.

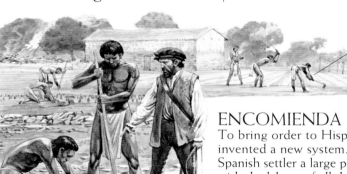

The Tainos had to work hard, growing food for their Spanish masters.

ENCOMIENDA
To bring order to Hispaniola, Columbus invented a new system. He gave each Spanish settler a large plot of land, together with the labour of all the Tainos living there. This was later called the *encomienda* ("in trust") system, because the land and Indians were held in the trust of the Spaniards.

Early October 1500 Columbus is sent back to Spain in chains.

21 August 1498 The ships reach Hispaniola.

5 August 1498 Columbus sets foot on the mainland.

5 August 1498 Giant wave hits the ships.

Spaniards hanged for rebelling against the Columbus brothers

BOBADILLA

Ferdinand and Isabella heard alarming reports of the chaos in Hispaniola. They sent Francisco de Bobadilla, a Spanish nobleman, to restore order. On 23 August 1500, he reached Santa Domingo, where Diego Columbus was in command. Bobadilla was shocked to find that Diego had just hanged seven Spanish rebels, and was about to hang five more.

Columbus never got over the humiliation of being chained up.

CHAINED IN IRONS

Won over by tales he heard from Columbus's enemies, Bobadilla arrested all three brothers and had them chained in irons. They were kept in prison for over a month, and then sent back to Spain by ship to stand trial.

Strange notions

COLUMBUS FOUND IT HARD to fit his newly discovered mainland – an unknown continent, not mentioned in the Bible – into his view of the world. He also developed some odd ideas about the shape of the Earth.

Pear-shaped world

Columbus, who was sick at the time, convinced himself that the stars were nearer to Earth than usual. He decided that he was sailing uphill and getting closer to the sky. This led him to conclude that the Earth was pear shaped.

Columbus thought he was sailing towards the stem of a pear-shaped Earth.

Paradise found?

The Earthly Paradise, described in the Book of Genesis, was the only land in the Bible whose location no one knew. Columbus believed that the Earthly Paradise lay on this newly discovered continent.

FACT file

• The ship's captain who took him back to Spain felt sorry for Columbus, and offered to remove the chains. Columbus refused, saying he would keep wearing his chains until the king and queen ordered their removal.

• Columbus wore his chains for more than three months.

• He wore the chains to show how he had been rewarded for his many services to Ferdinand and Isabella.

• For the rest of his life, Columbus kept the chains in his bedroom, to remind him of his treatment. He even asked to be buried with the chains.

DISGRACED

Bobadilla charged Columbus with oppressing the Spanish settlers and withholding gold from the king and queen. However, Columbus was never tried. Upset by the way that Bobadilla had treated him, Ferdinand and Isabella immediately pardoned Columbus. He never forgot the experience.

People were shocked by the sight of the chained Columbus returning in disgrace.

ACROSS THE WILD CARIBBEAN

FERDINAND AND ISABELLA WELCOMED Columbus at court, but refused to reinstate him as governor, since it was clear that he had made a mess of ruling Hispaniola. For months, Columbus bombarded them with complaints about his treatment. He made such a nuisance of himself that they agreed to let him lead one more voyage of exploration. In 1502, Columbus sailed with four ships across the Caribbean, searching for an ocean route to India. It was a terrible voyage across a wild, stormy sea.

Indian crocodiles?
On the mainland, Columbus saw alligators, which he presumed were crocodiles. Columbus may have taken this as an encouraging sign, because he knew from books he had read that there were crocodiles in India.

Pottery figure of Mayan woman

Mayas of the mainland
The ships encountered some Indians in a boat wearing beautifully woven clothes. They were Maya people from Central America. This was the first European contact with one of the rich civilizations of the mainland.

HURRICANE!
During the summer, the Caribbean can be ravaged by violent wind systems called hurricanes. Columbus reached the Caribbean in time for one of the worst hurricanes in years. His ships survived, but a fleet of 20 ships returning from Hispaniola to Spain was destroyed. Among the 500 dead was his old enemy, Bobadilla.

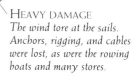

HEAVY DAMAGE
The wind tore at the sails. Anchors, rigging, and cables were lost, as were the rowing boats and many stores.

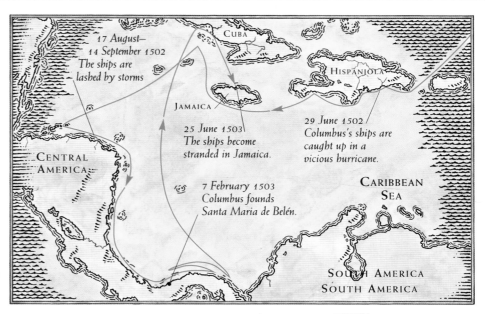

17 August – 14 September 1502
The ships are lashed by storms

CUBA

HISPANIOLA

JAMAICA

25 June 1503
The ships become stranded in Jamaica.

29 June 1502
Columbus's ships are caught up in a vicious hurricane.

CENTRAL AMERICA

7 February 1503
Columbus founds Santa Maria de Belén.

CARIBBEAN SEA

SOUTH AMERICA
SOUTH AMERICA

WATERSPOUT

On 13 December, the men were terrified by the sight of a waterspout – a column of water sucked up by an ocean whirlwind. To protect his fleet, Columbus held up a Bible and drew a cross in the air with his sword. The waterspout passed safely by.

Columbus was worried about his brother Bartolomé, who was on board Santiago, *the hardest ship of the fleet to sail.*

THE FOURTH VOYAGE

Columbus sailed down the coast of Central America, but failed to find a way through to India. His attempt to found a mainland settlement, Santa Maria de Bélen, also failed, when the settlers were attacked by Indians.

Shipworms
The Caribbean is home to wood-eating molluscs called shipworms. These worm-like creatures fastened themselves to Columbus's ships and munched away at their hulls. Soon the hulls were riddled with holes and rapidly filling with water.

Everyone could see that, despite their hard work, the ships were slowly sinking.

Columbus's son, Ferdinand, who had joined him for this voyage, worked as hard as anyone else.

Hell on the high seas

ALL HANDS TO THE PUMPS

With each day that passed, the ships took on more water – from the constant rain, from the waves lashing the sides of the ships, and through the holes bored by shipworms. The crews worked non-stop to pump and bail out the water, but they were fighting a losing battle.

AFTER MONTHS AT SEA, the ships became floating hells. The men were often soaked to the skin, hungry, and seasick. Many suffered from tropical fevers caused by insect bites.

Damp biscuits
The ship's biscuits became damp, soft, and crawling with maggots. They looked so disgusting that some of the men waited until dark to eat them.

Fleas and lice
The men grew so weak that they did not bother to keep clean. They were bitten by fleas and blood-sucking head and body lice.

Flies and maggots
The crews suffered from diarrhoea, caused by flies that feed on excrement and rotting meat and then transfer germs to fresh food.

Rats
Rats were a nuisance and a health risk on long voyages. They got into the food stores in the ships' holds, leaving behind foul-smelling urine and droppings.

STRANDED!

EYEWITNESS

"I am cut off…alone in my troubles, sick, each day expecting death, and surrounded by a million cruel and hostile savages…. if you have charity, truth, and justice, weep for me!"

Christopher Columbus, from a letter to Ferdinand and Isabella, 7 July 1503

TWO OF COLUMBUS'S WORM-EATEN SHIPS were leaking so badly that he had to abandon them. He headed north with the remaining pair, *Santiago* and *La Capitana*, towards Hispaniola. Carried off course by easterly winds and currents, Columbus found himself off Cuba. He tried to sail east to Hispaniola, but could make no progress against the winds. The ships were dangerously low in the water, and the crews were exhausted by constant work at the pumps. Columbus was forced to land in Jamaica, where he would be stranded for over a year.

HOUSEBOATS

On 25 June 1503, the ships were beached and turned into homes. Columbus's greatest worry was that the Jamaican Tainos might attack. To avoid provoking them, he ordered his men to stay on board, allowing only a few to go inland to trade for food. Penned up for months, the crews grew increasingly frustrated. Meanwhile, Columbus lay sick in his cabin.

FACT file

• Columbus set off on his fourth voyage with a crew of 143, including 55 boys. The large number of boys may have been due to the fact they could be paid less than grown men.

• More than 40 of the crew died on the voyage. They perished from sickness, drowning, and in battles with the Indians and each other.

• Only 25 of the survivors returned to Spain. The rest stayed in Hispaniola. They had done enough seafaring.

• Diego Mendez was so proud of his rescue mission that he had a canoe carved on his grave stone.

On the decks, the men built wooden huts, thatched with palm leaves.

Sails were fixed on the canoes.

SAILING FOR HELP
On 17 July 1503, Diego Mendez, a loyal follower of Columbus, set off for Hispaniola to get help. He took two Taino canoes, manned by seven crewmen and ten Indians.

PORRAS REVOLTS
Francisco de Porras, captain of *Santiago*, spread a rumour that Columbus did not intend to leave Jamaica, but wanted to keep everybody there to die with him. On 2 January 1504, he convinced 48 men to join him in a mutiny. The mutineers took ten Taino canoes and headed for Hispaniola.

The mutineers robbed Taino villages as they rowed along the coast towards Hispaniola.

The Tainos panicked as the Moon, turned blood-red by the eclipse, began to disappear.

A CUNNING PLAN

When the Tainos stopped bringing food to the ships, Columbus came up with a clever plan to scare them into obedience. He knew from an astronomy book that there would be an eclipse of the Moon on 29 February. He told the Tainos that he would punish them that night by asking God to put out the light of the Moon. The trick worked, and the terrified Tainos brought all the food they could find.

SWORD FIGHT

The mutineers tried and failed three times to reach Hispaniola in their canoes. Porras now accused Columbus of using witchcraft to keep them in Jamaica. On 19 May, the mutineers marched back towards the ships to fight. Bartolomé Columbus went to meet them with 50 armed men. A fierce battle followed, which Bartolomé won. Porras was captured, and the mutineers surrendered.

The men fought mainly with swords, since there was little gunpowder left.

Columbus's men were fitter and better fed than the mutineers.

After a year and five days on Jamaica, the men were overjoyed to see Mendez's ship.

RESCUED AT LAST

Although Diego Mendez had reached Hispaniola by August 1503, it was several months before he was able to buy a ship and load it with supplies to send to Columbus. The ship arrived at the end of June 1504, nearly a year since Mendez had left with his canoes. Columbus told Mendez that the day of his rescue was the most joyful in his life. He had expected to die in Jamaica.

Disappointment in death

COLUMBUS RETURNED TO SPAIN in November 1504. He was now an old man, his health ruined by his long voyages. He spent his last months pleading unsuccessfully to have his rights restored. He died on 20 May 1506. With his voyages of exploration, he had changed the course of world history. Yet, to the day he died, Columbus never realized that he had not reached Asia.

Monks say prayers over the dying Columbus, while his sons look on

VOYAGES OF EXPLORATION

BY THE LATE 1490S, Columbus's voyages had inspired other explorers to set off across the Atlantic. At first, they shared Columbus's hope that they would reach the Indies. But gradually they realized that the lands across the Atlantic had nothing to do with Asia. They had found two continents previously unknown to Europeans, later named North and South America.

John Cabot
Like Columbus, Cabot was a Genoese seafarer. In 1497, he sailed west in search of the Indies, backed by King Henry VII of England. He reached North America, and believed it to be China. In 1498, he set off on another voyage, but was never heard from again.

CABOT LEAVING BRISTOL, ENGLAND, ON 20 MAY 1497

Vespucci and the "New World"
Amerigo Vespucci made two voyages to the mainland, in 1499 and in 1501. Vespucci realized that the mainland was not part of the Indies. He wrote that it was a "New World", which he claimed to have discovered. This impressed a German mapmaker, who suggested the name "America" in Vespucci's honour.

LAND BARRIER
Europeans were shocked to learn that a vast land barrier blocked any sea route to the wealth of the Indies. But when Balboa walked across America at its narrowest part (Panama), it was hoped that this was a narrow continent, and the Indies might be just a short sea journey beyond. Magellan's voyage across the Pacific soon disproved this theory.

Map labels: Cabot 1497 · EUROPE · Vespucci 1499~1500 · AFRICA · PACIFIC OCEAN · NORTH AMERICA · Balboa 1513 · CARIBBEAN SEA · PACIFIC OCEAN · PANAMA · EQUATOR · SOUTH AMERICA · ATLANTIC OCEAN · Magellan 1519

KEY TO MAP:
CABOT _____
VESPUCCI _____
BALBOA _____
MAGELLAN _____

Balboa reaches the Pacific
In 1513, Vasco Núñez de Balboa led an expedition across the American mainland, and became the first European to see the Pacific Ocean. Wearing armour and waving his sword, he waded into the water and declared that this sea and all its islands now belonged to Spain. However, Balboa did not suspect that the Pacific is the world's largest ocean, covering a third of the Earth's surface.

Ferdinand Magellan
In 1519, Ferdinand Magellan led a Spanish fleet in search of a strait (passage of water) through America to the Pacific. He found a strait, at the tip of South America, and then discovered the true size of the Pacific. It took Magellan almost four months to reach the Philippines, where he was killed. Only one of his four ships, the *Vittoria*, made it back to Spain. After three years at sea, *Vittoria* became the first ship to sail around the world.

Improvements in navigation

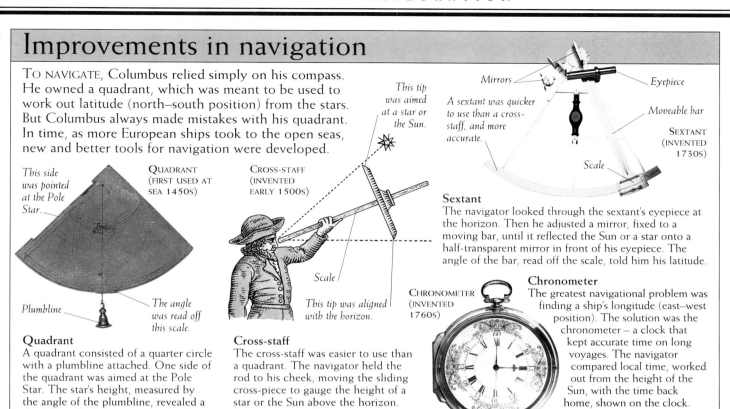

TO NAVIGATE, Columbus relied simply on his compass. He owned a quadrant, which was meant to be used to work out latitude (north–south position) from the stars. But Columbus always made mistakes with his quadrant. In time, as more European ships took to the open seas, new and better tools for navigation were developed.

This side was pointed at the Pole Star.

QUADRANT (FIRST USED AT SEA 1450S)

CROSS-STAFF (INVENTED EARLY 1500S)

This tip was aimed at a star or the Sun.

A sextant was quicker to use than a cross-staff, and more accurate.

Mirrors — *Eyepiece*

Moveable bar

SEXTANT (INVENTED 1730S)

Scale

Plumbline

The angle was read off this scale.

Scale

This tip was aligned with the horizon.

Sextant
The navigator looked through the sextant's eyepiece at the horizon. Then he adjusted a mirror, fixed to a moving bar, until it reflected the Sun or a star onto a half-transparent mirror in front of his eyepiece. The angle of the bar, read off the scale, told him his latitude.

CHRONOMETER (INVENTED 1760S)

Chronometer
The greatest navigational problem was finding a ship's longitude (east–west position). The solution was the chronometer – a clock that kept accurate time on long voyages. The navigator compared local time, worked out from the height of the Sun, with the time back home, shown on the clock. The difference told him how far the ship had sailed east or west.

Quadrant
A quadrant consisted of a quarter circle with a plumbline attached. One side of the quadrant was aimed at the Pole Star. The star's height, measured by the angle of the plumbline, revealed a ship's latitude. But it was very hard to use on the rolling deck of a ship.

Cross-staff
The cross-staff was easier to use than a quadrant. The navigator held the rod to his cheek, moving the sliding cross-piece to gauge the height of a star or the Sun above the horizon. Measurements of latitude were read off a scale along the staff's edge.

THE WORLD'S TRUE SIZE
Magellan's voyage revealed just how wrong Columbus had been in his ideas of geography. The world was much larger than Columbus suspected, and there was no short-cut to the Indies. The Americas and the Pacific Ocean stood in the way.

Compare this with the world map on pages 6–7, made only about 60 years earlier. It is much more like the maps you can find in modern atlases.

This line shows the route taken by Magellan's ship Vittoria in 1519-22, on her historic voyage around the world.

On reaching the Philippines, Magellan got caught up in a local war. He was killed in a battle on 27 April 1521. Magellan had set off with 270 men. Only 17 returned to Spain on Vittoria.

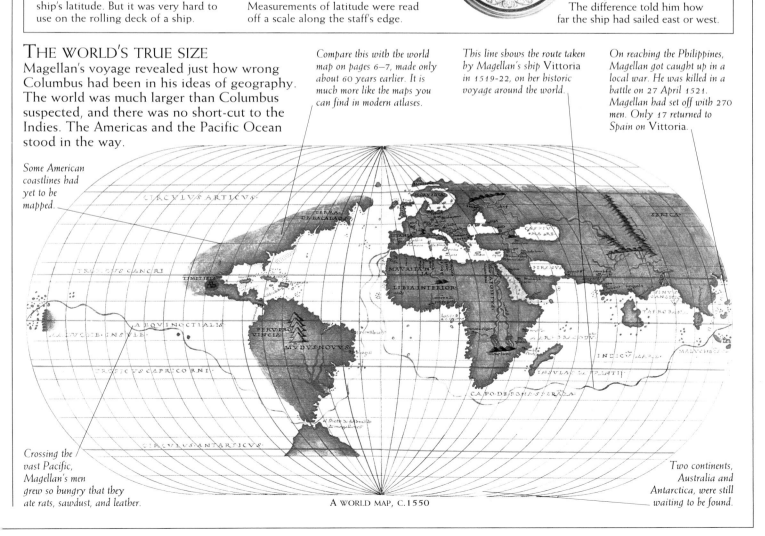

Some American coastlines had yet to be mapped.

Crossing the vast Pacific, Magellan's men grew so hungry that they ate rats, sawdust, and leather.

Two continents, Australia and Antarctica, were still waiting to be found.

A WORLD MAP, C.1550

CONQUISTADORES

The Aztecs welcomed Cortes to Mexico with valuable gifts.

Spanish troops

Hernán Cortés

SPAIN NEVER DISCOVERED A short cut to the riches of Asia. However, Spaniards who followed Columbus to the American mainland found civilizations that were much wealthier than the Tainos of Hispaniola. In the 16th century, these mainland civilizations were all destroyed by Spanish *conquistadores* ("conquerors").

FALL OF THE AZTEC EMPIRE
In 1519, Hernán Cortés led a Spanish army to Mexico. Moctezuma, the Aztec ruler, thought Cortés might be a god, so he treated him well. It was a terrible mistake: two years later, the Spaniards had laid waste to Tenochtitlán, the Aztec's great capital city, and the empire was in ruins.

Aztecs, Maya, and Incas
The conquistadores were amazed to find three great civilizations on the American mainland: the Aztec empire of Mexico, the Inca empire of Peru, and the Mayan kingdoms of Central America. Each civilization was conquered in turn.

Bodies were hurled down the temple steps.

Aztec religion
The Spaniards were horrified to learn that the Aztecs captured prisoners in war and cut their hearts out to offer to the gods. The Aztecs believed that the Sun would not rise if they did not make these sacrifices. This picture shows a sacrifice to Huitzilopochtli, god of war.

An Aztec, now made to wear European clothes, brings his books to be burned by the friars.

Friars were Spanish holy men.

Burning the gods
Spanish friars followed the conquistadores to the Americas, preaching the Christian religion. The friars destroyed all the images of Aztec gods, convinced that these were devils. They ransacked Aztec and Maya libraries, burning books and often their owners as well.

Writing and record keeping

THE AZTECS, INCAS, AND MAYA each invented complex methods of keeping records. These helped them to govern their subjects and collect tribute from conquered peoples. The Aztecs and Maya also used their writing systems to keep track of events in sacred calendars.

Inca quipu
The Incas had no writing, yet they were able to keep complicated records using lengths of coloured knotted string, called quipus.

Mayan codex
The Maya developed a complete alphabet, with picture-signs to represent different sounds. Mayan codices (books) were used to record religious information. Only four codices survived the Spanish conquest.

Aztec calendar stone
The Aztecs used a simple form of writing, with pictures standing for dates and events. This stone, covered with Aztec dates, shows the creation of the universe.

PIZARRO AND THE INCAS

Francisco Pizarro led a tiny force of 180 Spaniards to Peru in 1532. He arrived when the Inca empire was weak due to civil war. In a bold move, Pizarro captured the Inca emperor, Atahualpa, in front of his own army and demanded a roomful of gold as ransom. Atahualpa paid the ransom, but Pizarro had him strangled anyway.

This painted wooden beaker shows an Inca noble in a headdress, walking behind his conqueror, a Spanish trumpeter.

Lost city of the Incas

The Incas were expert stonemasons who built mighty cities and fortresses out of huge stone blocks. This is Machu Pichu, an Inca mountain stronghold 2,400 m (7,875 ft) above sea level. It was never found by the Spaniards, yet it was abandoned around the time of the conquest. Half the Inca population had died from European smallpox, which swept through South America, even before Pizarro's arrival.

Machu Pichu was only discovered in 1911.

CONQUEST OF THE MAYA

The Maya were the oldest mainland civilization, and they were already in decline when the Spaniards arrived. Yet they put up the strongest resistance to the conquistadores. They lived in many kingdoms, which had to be conquered one by one. The last Maya stronghold fell in 1697.

MAGICIAN'S PYRAMID, UXMAL, MEXICO

MAYAN TEMPLES
Like the Aztecs, the Maya built their temples on top of huge stone pyramids. This one is at Uxmal, in Mexico. Like many Maya cities, Uxmal was abandoned 400 years before the conquistadores arrived.

The Magician's Pyramid is 38 m (117 ft) high.

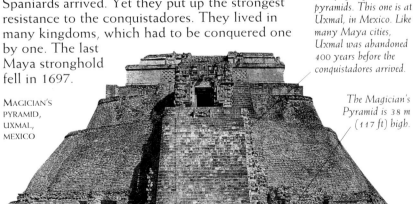

After Columbus

THE PERIOD OF AMERICAN HISTORY before the Spanish conquest is known as "Precolumbian" (before Columbus). Columbus's voyages, which led to the conquests, changed almost everything in the Americas. The conquistadores introduced new animals, such as horses, sheep, pigs, and cattle; new food crops, such as wheat; tools made from iron and steel; wheeled transport; and, of course, the Spanish language.

Religious legacy

The Spaniards made the native peoples give up their old religions and become Christians. This cathedral, in Mexico City, was built on top of the ruins of Aztec temples torn down by conquistadores. Mexico City itself is a European-style capital, built on the site of Tenochtitlán.

What survived?

Despite the changes, many aspects of Native American daily life survived the Spanish conquest. Women in Mexico and Central America still cook meals, such as maize tortillas, which were eaten by the Aztecs and the Maya. Traditional skills and crafts live on, too: cloth is still woven using a "backstrap loom", just as it has been for many thousands of years.

GOLDEN REWARD

The mainland peoples used gold for jewellery and ornaments. These were melted down by the conquistadores and sent back to Spain. American gold and silver made Spain rich and powerful, and was used to finance European wars.

Beads decorated with spirals

Necklace

This gold necklace was found buried inside the Aztecs' Great Temple at Tenochtitlán.

Nose plug

A Mexican gold nose plug – one of the few not melted down by the conquistadores.

Doubloons carried the Christian Cross.

Spanish doubloons

Much of the Aztec and Inca gold was made into coins like these doubloons, which are decorated with the royal lion and castle of Spain.

Index

Acknowledgments

The publisher would like to thank the following for their kind permission to reproduce their images:

Position key: c=centre; b=bottom; l=left; r=right; t=top

AKG London: 10tl, 26bl, 44bc; Bibliotheque Nationale 8br, 9tr; British Library 11t; Erich Lessing 29br; Sevilla Biblioteca Columbina 12cl; Veintimilla 47cl; Bridgeman Art Library, London / New York: Biblioteca Nacional, Madrid, Spain 46tr; British Library 6–7, 9b; Library of Congress, Washington 35 cr; British Library, London: 34cl, 45b; British Museum: 8bl, 12tl, 15cr, 47br; INAH 40bl, 46bl; Corbis UK Ltd: 36–37; Bettmann 32cl; The Art Archive: Palazzo Farnese Caprarola/Dagli Orti 44br; Mary Evans Picture Library: 18–19dps, 39tl; De Lorgues 43br; Glasgow University Library: Ms Hunter 46cr; INAH: 40bl, 46bl; Katz Pictures: The Mansell Collection 14bl, 15tl, 30–31; Museum of Mankind: 47t; Museum of Order St. John: 35c (above); Peter Newark's Pictures: 44cl; Ernest Board 44tr; National Maritime Museum: 11tc, 12br, 41bc, 45tr, 45cr; N.H.P.A.: Kevin Schafer 39cr; Robin Wigington, Arbour Antiques: 35tl; Scala Group S.p.A.: Biblioteca Nazionale Firenze 46c; Science Photo Library: Eye of Science 33tl; Wallace Collection: 35cl (above); Warwick Castle: 35tc.